HAL•LEONARD

GUITAR
PLAY-ALONG®

ROBERT JOHNSON

T0083892

Robert Johnson Studio Portrait
Hooks Bros., Memphis, c. 1935
© 1989 Delta Haze Corporation
All Rights Reserved Used by Permission

ISBN 978-1-4584-1489-2

HAL•LEONARD®
CORPORATION
7777 W. BLUEMOUND RD. P.O. BOX 13819 MILWAUKEE, WI 53213

Visit Hal Leonard Online at
www.halleonard.com

CONTENTS

GUITAR NOTATION LEGEND

THE MUSICAL STAFF shows pitches and rhythms and is divided by bar lines into measures. Pitches are named after the first seven letters of the alphabet.

TABLATURE graphically represents the guitar fingerboard. Each horizontal line represents a string, and each number represents a fret.

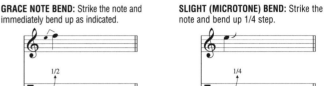

Notes:

Strings:
high E B G D A low E

4th string, 2nd fret

1st & 2nd strings open, played together

open D chord

HALF-STEP BEND: Strike the note and bend up 1/2 step.

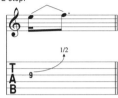

WHOLE-STEP BEND: Strike the note and bend up one step.

GRACE NOTE BEND: Strike the note and immediately bend up as indicated.

SLIGHT (MICROTONE) BEND: Strike the note and bend up 1/4 step.

BEND AND RELEASE: Strike the note and bend up as indicated, then release back to the original note. Only the first note is struck.

PRE-BEND: Bend the note as indicated, then strike it.

VIBRATO: The string is vibrated by rapidly bending and releasing the note with the fretting hand.

PALM MUTING: The note is partially muted by the pick hand lightly touching the string(s) just before the bridge.

HAMMER-ON: Strike the first (lower) note with one finger, then sound the higher note (on the same string) with another finger by fretting it without picking.

PULL-OFF: Place both fingers on the notes to be sounded. Strike the first note and without picking, pull the finger off to sound the second (lower) note.

LEGATO SLIDE: Strike the first note and then slide the same fret-hand finger up or down to the second note. The second note is not struck.

SHIFT SLIDE: Same as legato slide, except the second note is struck.

TRILL: Very rapidly alternate between the notes indicated by continuously hammering on and pulling off.

TAPPING: Hammer ("tap") the fret indicated with the pick-hand index or middle finger and pull off to the note fretted by the fret hand.

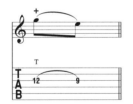

NATURAL HARMONIC: Strike the note while the fret-hand lightly touches the string directly over the fret indicated.

PINCH HARMONIC: The note is fretted normally and a harmonic is produced by adding the edge of the thumb or the tip of the index finger of the pick hand to the normal pick attack.

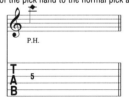

TREMOLO PICKING: The note is picked as rapidly and continuously as possible.

VIBRATO BAR DIVE AND RETURN: The pitch of the note or chord is dropped a specified number of steps (in rhythm), then returned to the original pitch.

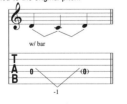

VIBRATO BAR SCOOP: Depress the bar just before striking the note, then quickly release the bar.

VIBRATO BAR DIP: Strike the note and then immediately drop a specified number of steps, then release back to the original pitch.

Additional Musical Definitions

 (accent) • Accentuate note (play it louder).

(staccato) • Play the note short.

D.S. al Coda • Go back to the sign (%), then play until the measure marked "*To Coda,*" then skip to the section labelled "**Coda.**"

D.C. al Fine • Go back to the beginning of the song and play until the measure marked "*Fine*" (end).

Fill • Label used to identify a brief melodic figure which is to be inserted into the arrangement.

N.C. • Harmony is implied.

 • Repeat measures between signs.

 • When a repeated section has different endings, play the first ending only the first time and the second ending only the second time.

Come On in My Kitchen

Words and Music by Robert Johnson

Open G tuning:
(low to high) D-G-D-G-B-D

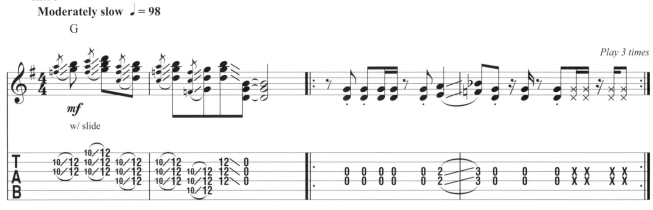

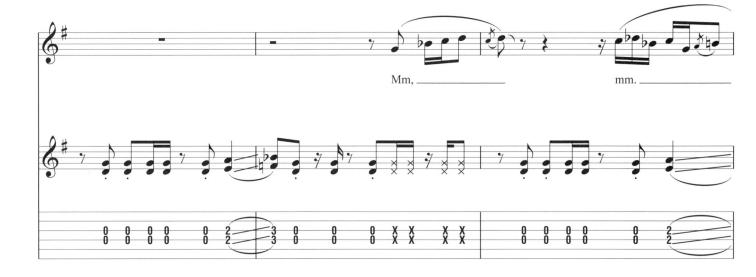

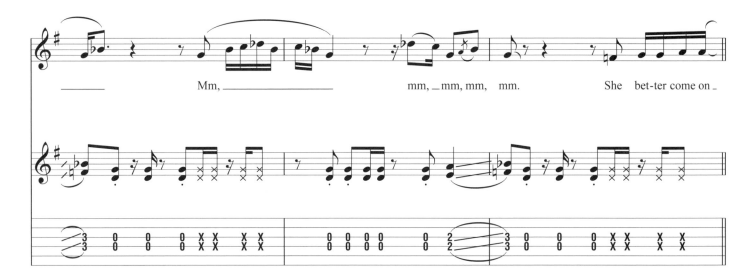

Chorus

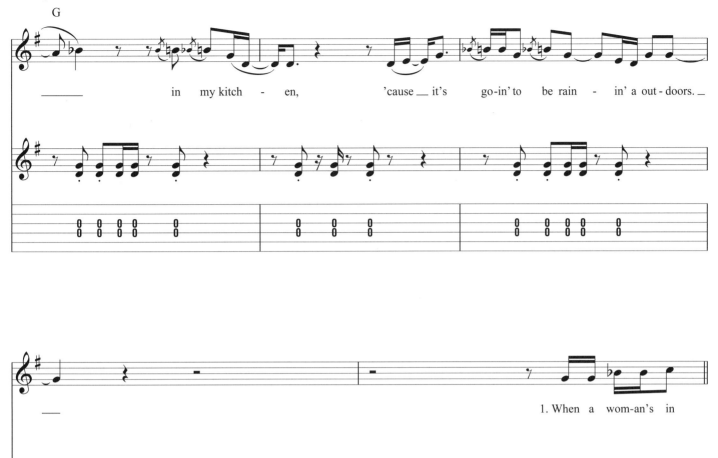

_____ in my kitch - en, 'cause __ it's go-in' to be rain - in' a out - doors. _

_____ 1. When a wom-an's in

w/o slide   w/ slide

Verse

trou - ble __ ev - 'ry - bod - y throws her ___ down. _ You search for your

2., 3. _See additional lyrics_

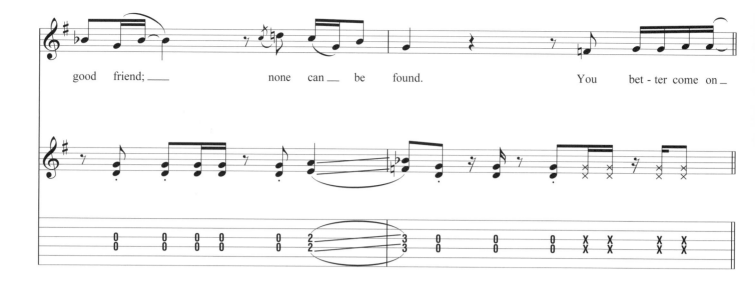

good friend; ___ none can ___ be found. You bet - ter come on ___

Chorus
G

___ in my kitch - en, 'cause ___ it's go - in' to be rain - in' a out - doors. ___

To Coda ⊕

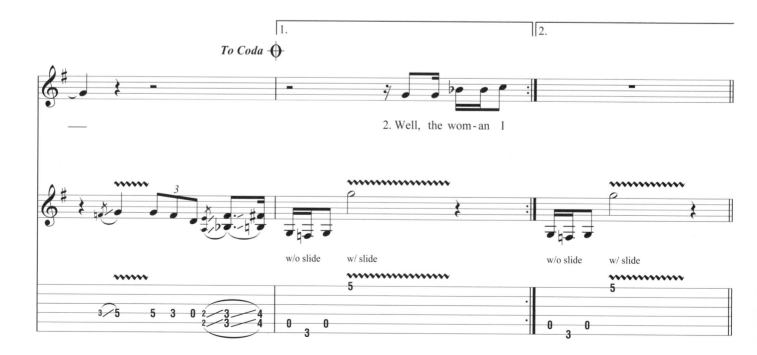

___   2. Well, the wom - an I

w/o slide   w/ slide   w/o slide   w/ slide

Interlude

Oh, the wind do howl. _ Can't you hear the wind _ howl?

D.S. al Coda

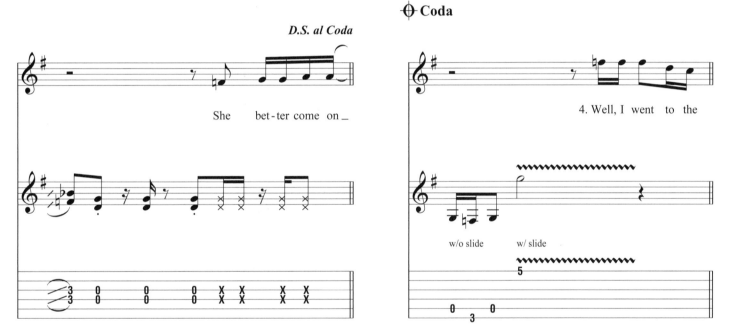

She bet-ter come on _

⊕ **Coda**

4. Well, I went to the

w/o slide   w/ slide

Verse

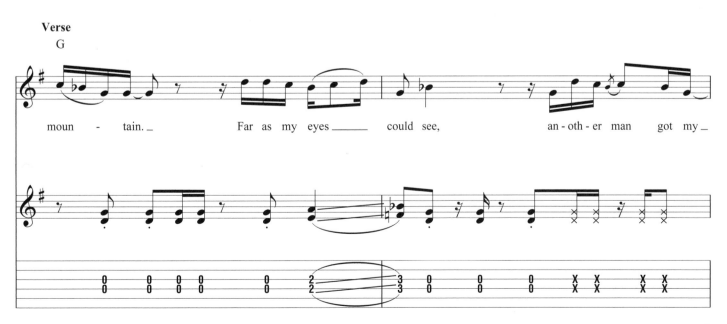

moun - tain. _ Far as my eyes_____ could see, an - oth - er man got my _

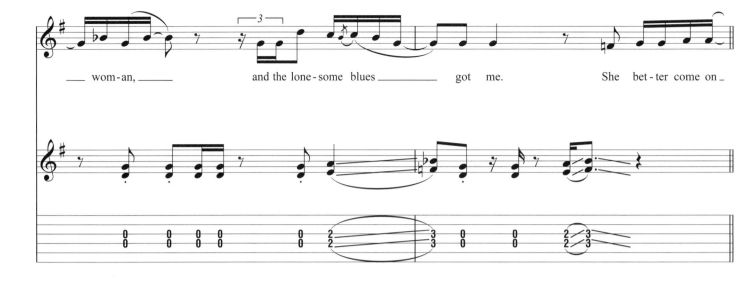

_____ wom-an, _____ and the lone-some blues _____ got me. She bet-ter come on

Chorus
G

_____ in my kitch-en, 'cause __ it's go-in' to be rain - in' a out-doors. _

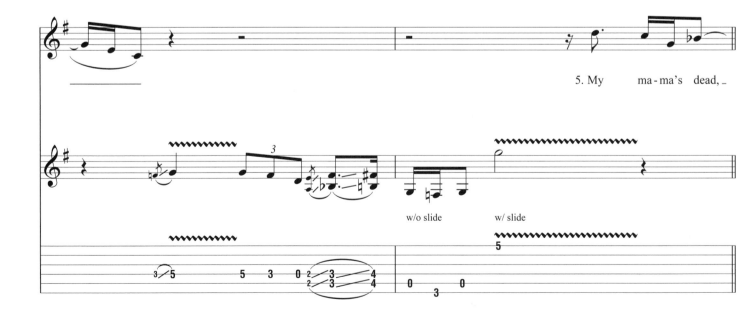

_____ 5. My ma-ma's dead, _

w/o slide   w/ slide

Verse

pa - pa's no-where to be. _____   I ain't got no -

bod - y   to love and care _ for me. _____   You bet - ter come on _

Chorus

_____   in my kitch - en, _   'cause _ it's

go-in' to   be   rain -   in' a   out-doors. _____   She bet-ter come on __

Outro-Chorus
G

_____   in my kitch - en, ___   'cause ___ it's

go-in' to   be   rain -   in' a   out-doors. _____   Oh, _____   yeah,

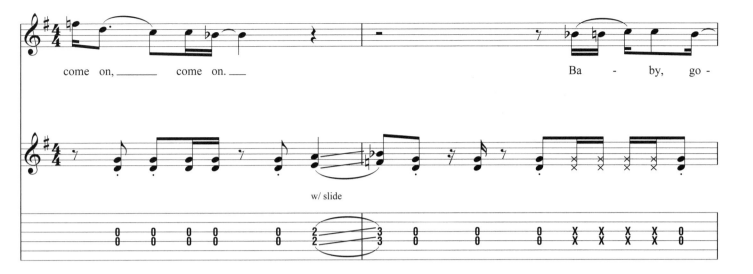

come on, _____ come on. _____ Ba - by, go-

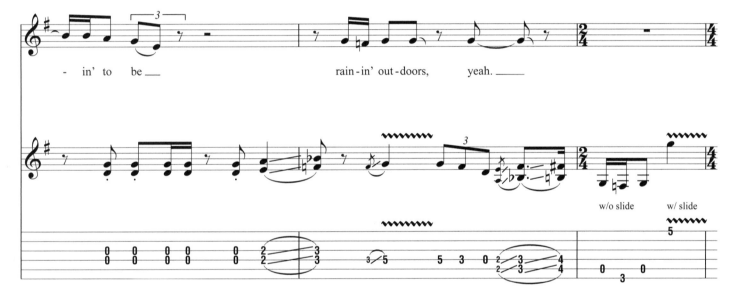

- in' to be _____ rain-in' out-doors, yeah. _____

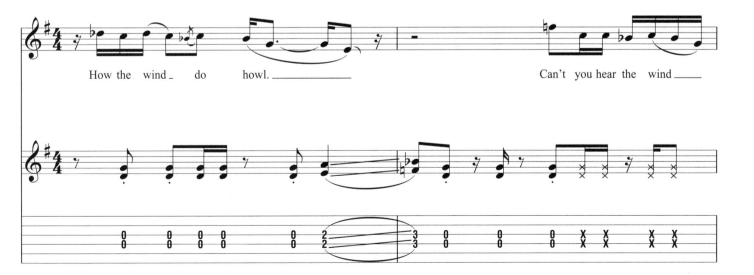

How the wind _ do howl. _____ Can't you hear the wind _____

ba - by, come ___ on, 'cause it's

go - in' to be rain - in' a out - doors. ___ Bet ter,

w/o slide   w/ slide

hoo.   Ba - by, ba - by, it's

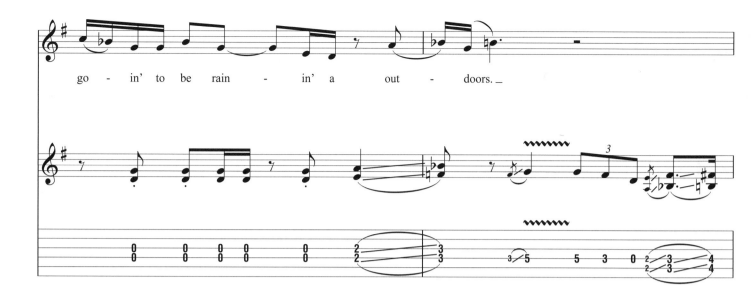

go - in' to be rain - in' a out - doors. _

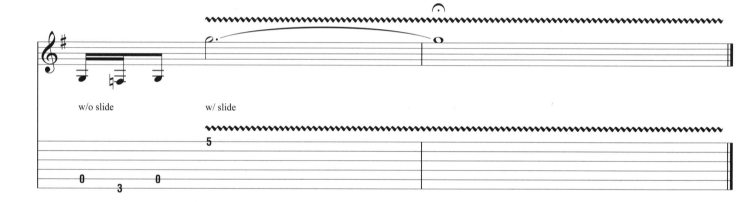

w/o slide   w/ slide

Additional Lyrics

2. Well, the woman I love stole from my best friend.
   Some joker got lucky; stole her back again.

3. Well, the woman I love I crave to see.
   She's up the country; she won't write to me.

Cross Road Blues
(Crossroads)

Words and Music by Robert Johnson

Intro

Moderately fast Rock ♩ = 130

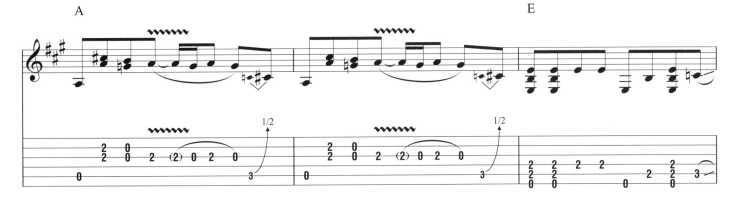

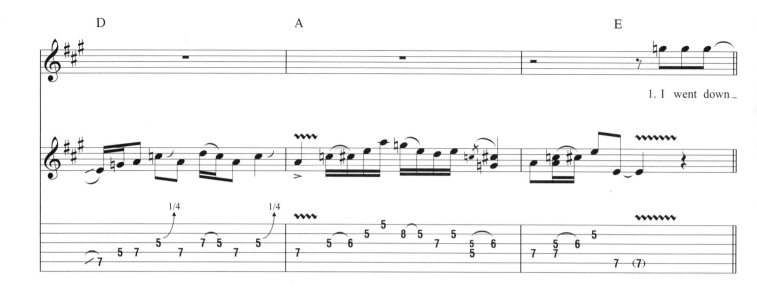

1. I went down

Verse

— to the cross - roads, fell down — on my knee. —

2., 3. *See additional lyrics*

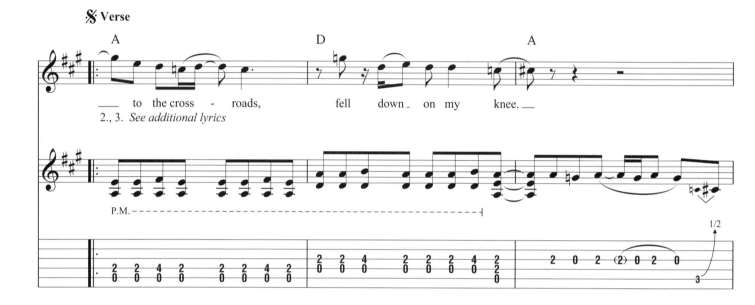

Down — to the cross - roads, fell down — on my knee. —

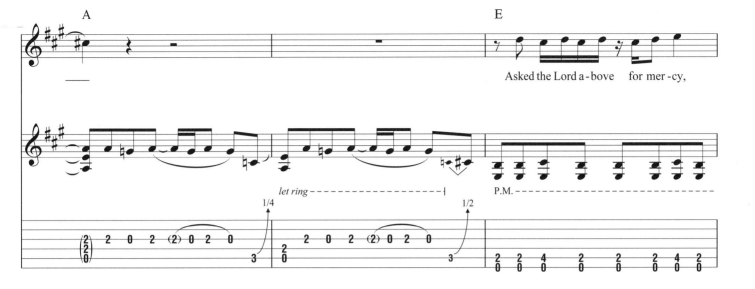

Asked the Lord a-bove for mer-cy,

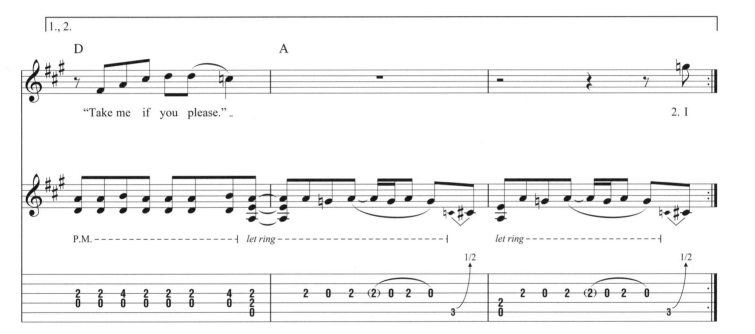

"Take me if you please." _

2. I

on the riv-er side. _____

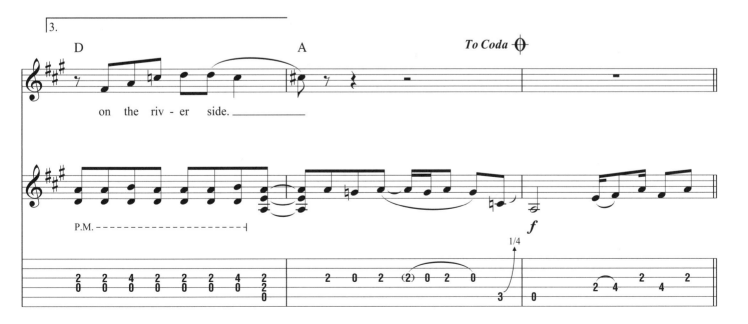

To Coda ⊕

ƒ

Guitar Solo

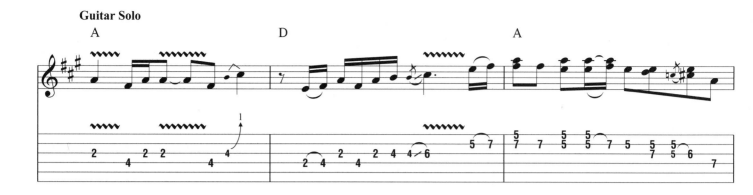

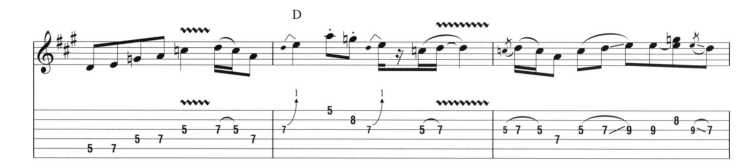

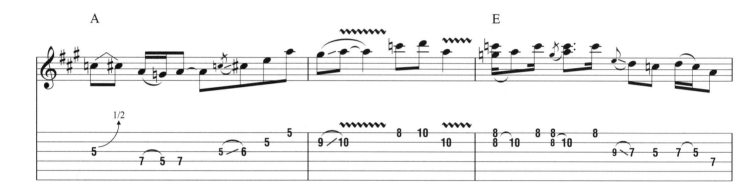

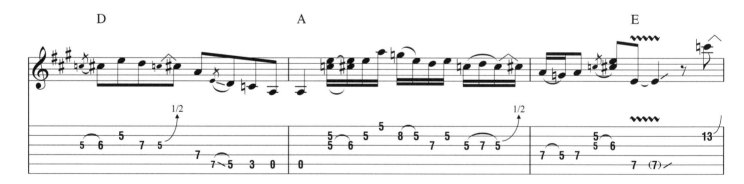

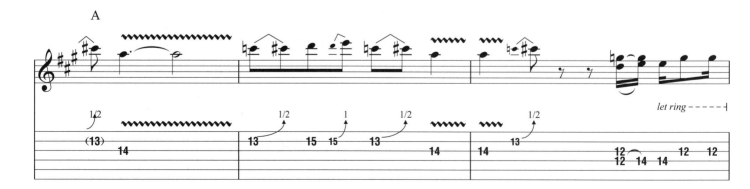

20

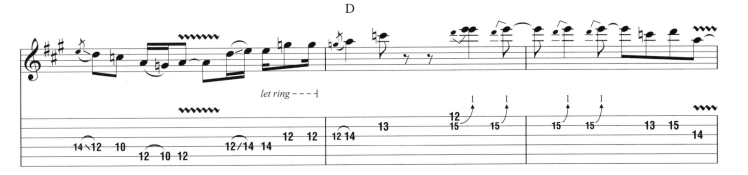

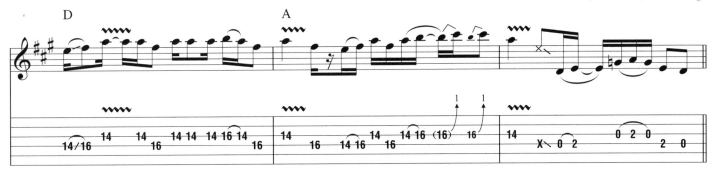

D.S. al Coda
(3rd Verse, 3rd ending)

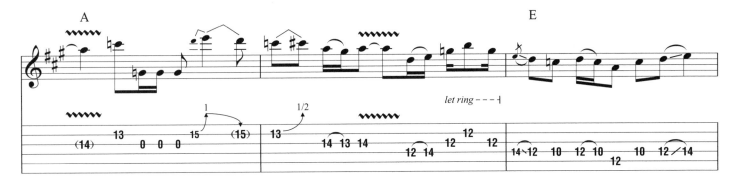

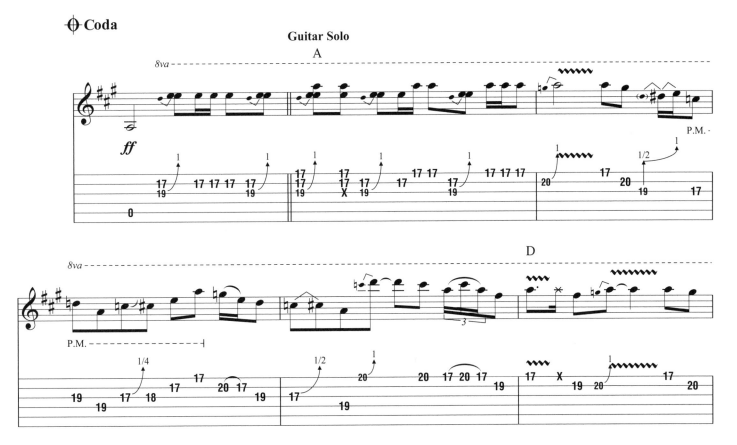

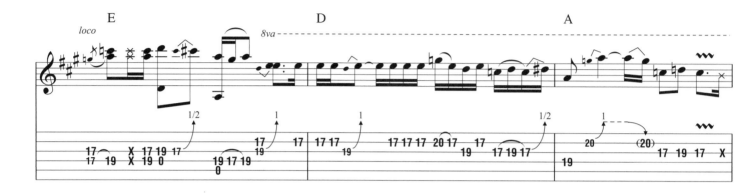

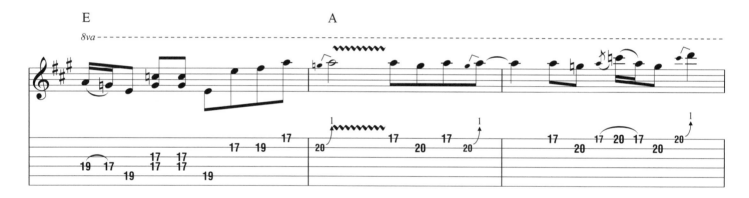

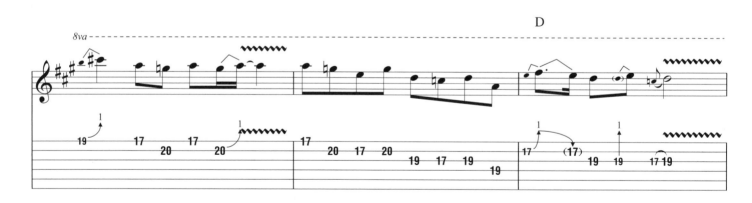

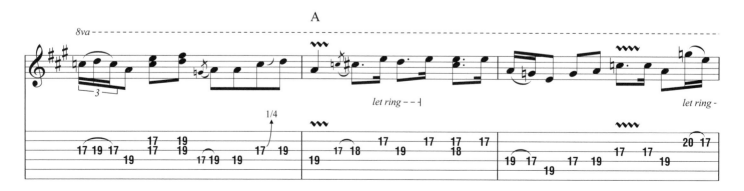

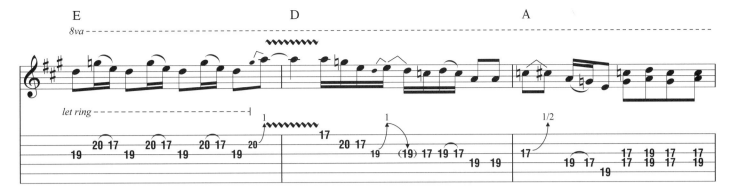

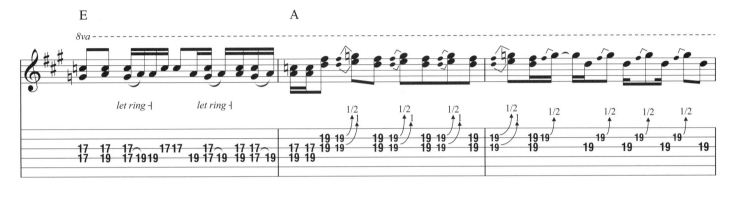

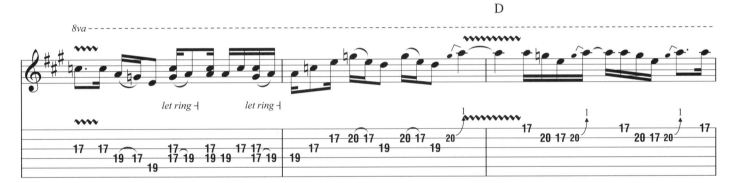

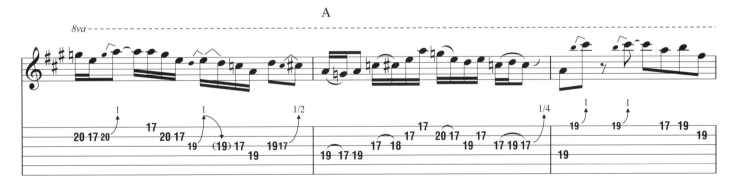

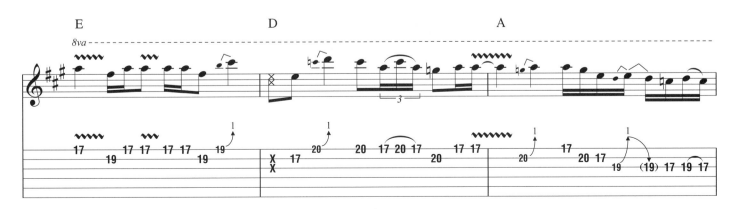

Outro-Verse

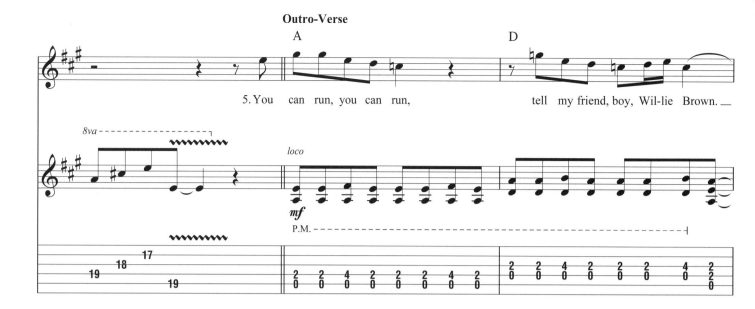

5. You can run, you can run, tell my friend, boy, Wil-lie Brown. ___

Run, ___ you can run, ___

tell my ___ friend, boy, Wil-lie Brown. ___ And I'm

stand-in' at the cross - road, be - lieve I'm __ sink - in' down.

Free time

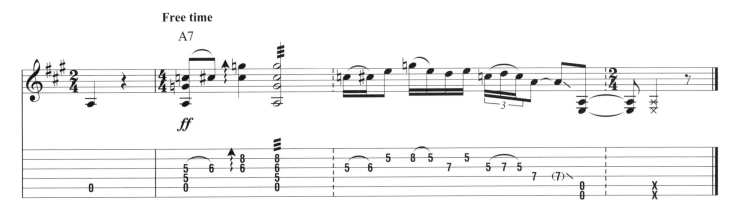

Additional Lyrics

2. I went down to the crossroad, tried to flag a ride.
   Down to the crossroad, tried to flag a ride.
   Nobody seemed to know me. Ev'rybody passed me by.

3. When I'm goin' down to Rosedale, take my rider by my side.
   Goin' down to Rosedale, take my rider by my side.
   We can still barrelhouse, baby, on the riverside.

Love in Vain Blues

Words and Music by Robert Johnson

Capo III

Intro
Slow Blues ♩. = 60

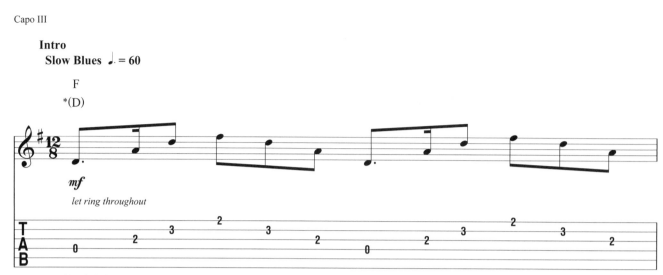

*Symbols in parentheses represent chord names respective to capoed guitar.
Symbols above reflect actual sounding chords. Capoed fret is "0" in tab.

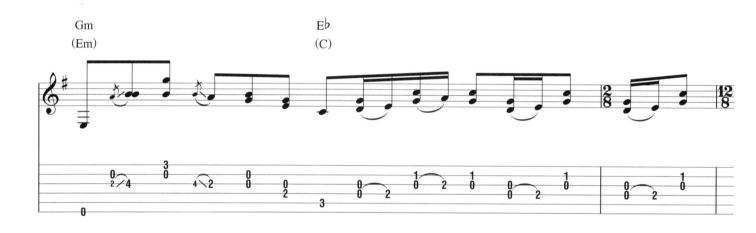

Verse

lowed her _____ to the sta - tion _

with a suit-case   in my hand. _____   Yeah, I

fol-lowed her to the sta - tion _   with a suit-case _   in my hand. _

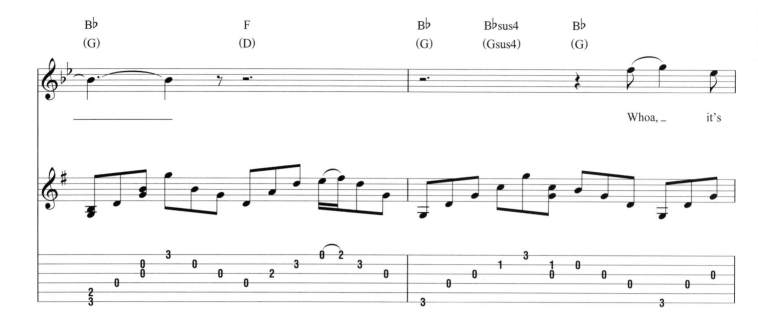

Whoa, ___ it's

hard to tell, it's ___ hard to tell ___ when all ___ your love's _____ in vain. ___

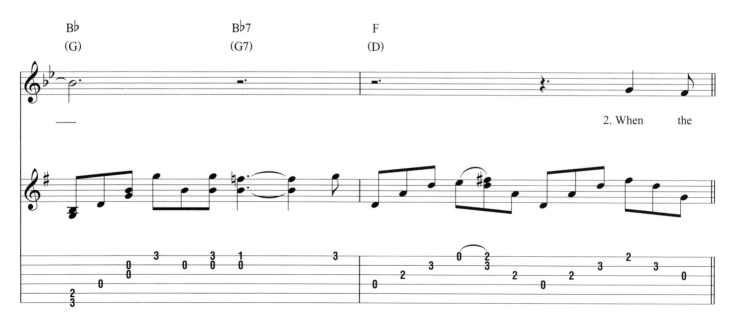

___ 2. When the

Verse

train _____ come in the sta - tion, _

I looked her in the eye. _____ Well, the

train come in _ the sta - tion, _ and I looked her in the eye. _____

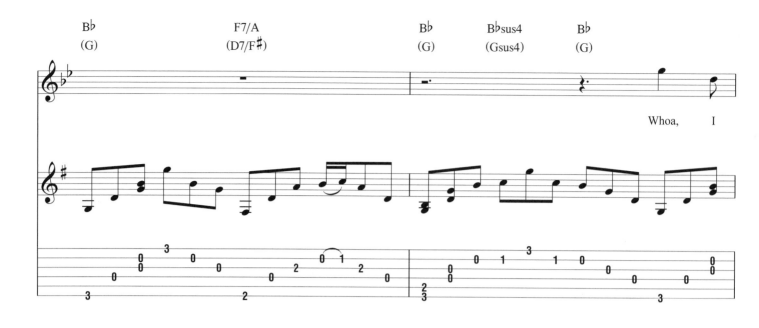

Whoa, I

felt so sad, so lone - some that I could not help but

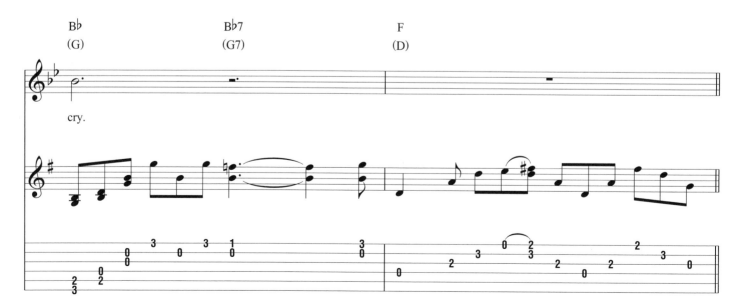

cry.

Mandolin Solo

B♭
(G)

Hey, _____ hey. _____

B♭7
(G7)

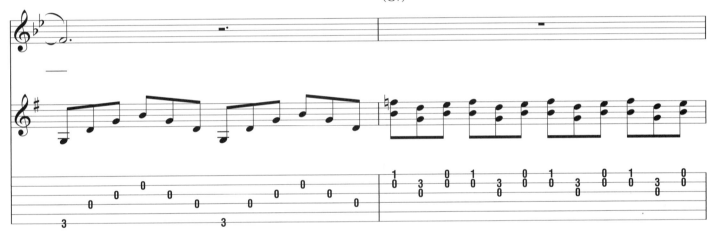

E♭   F7/A
(C)   (D7/F♯)

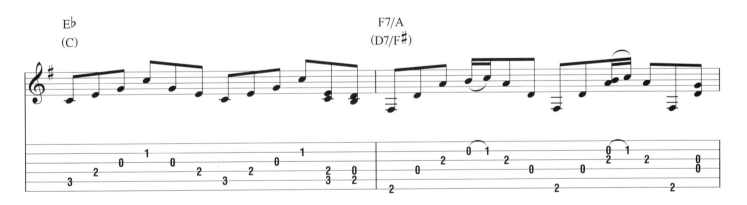

B♭   F7/A   B♭   B♭sus4   B♭
(G)   (D7/F♯)   (G)   (Gsus4)   (G)

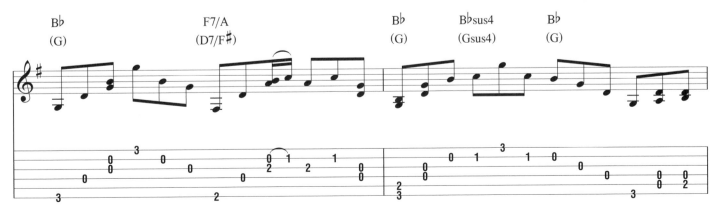

31

Outro

All _____ my __ love _____ was _____ in __ vain.

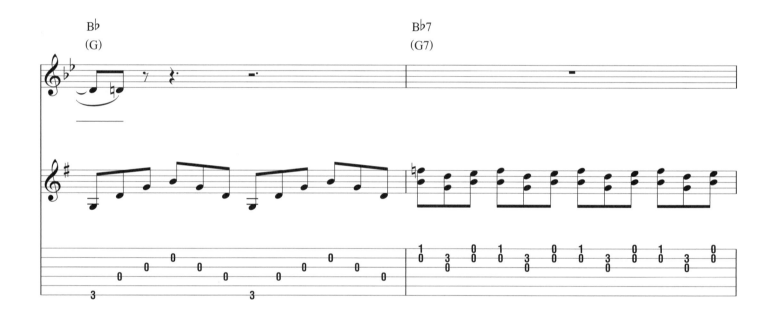

Oo, _____ hey. _____ Hey, _____ hey. __

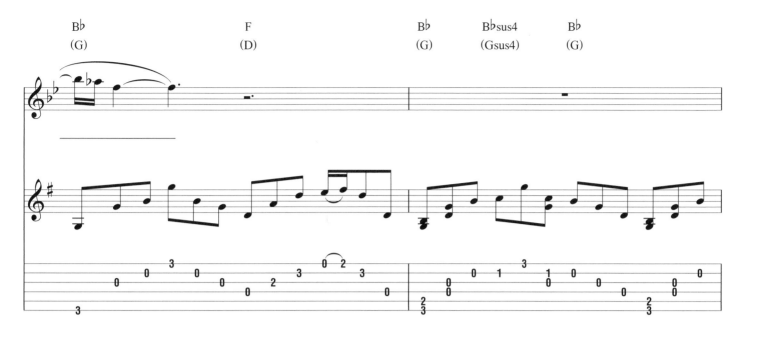

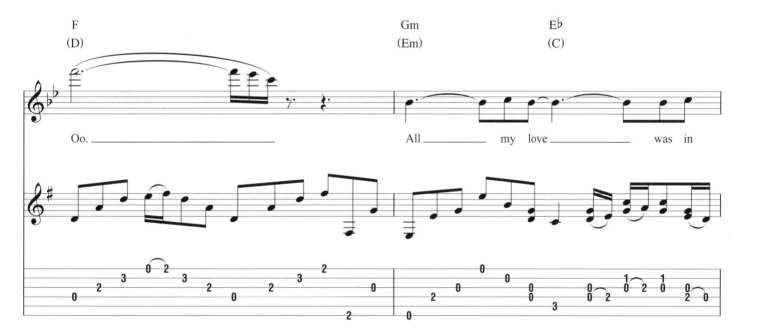

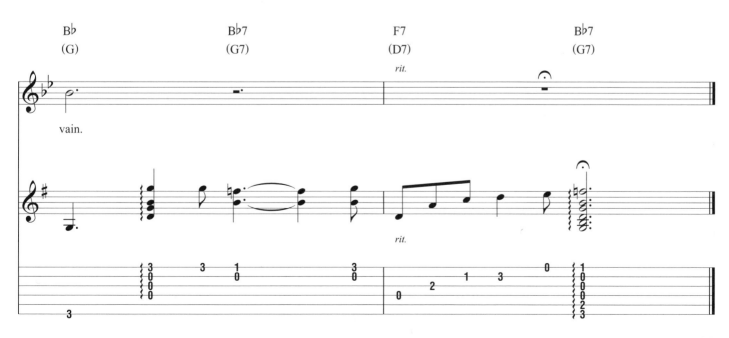

Ramblin' on My Mind

Words and Music by Robert Johnson

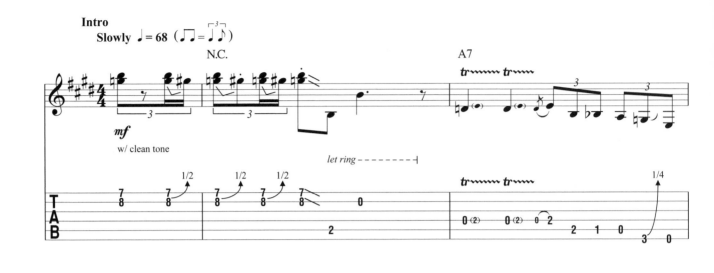

*w/ pick & fingers, where applicable.

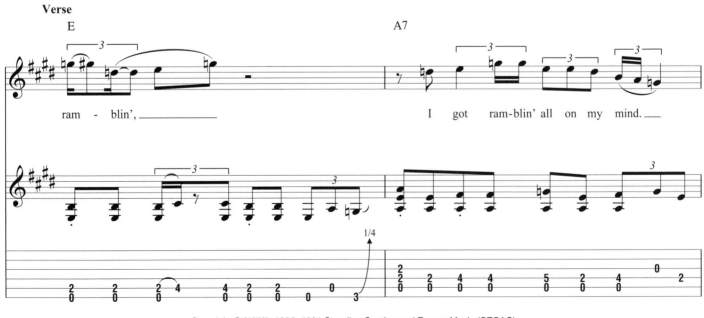

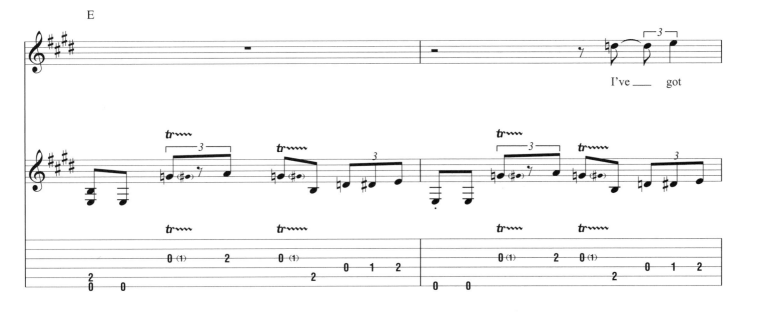

I've ___ got

ram - blin', ___   I've got   ram-blin' all   on my mind. _____

___   Is ___ to leave

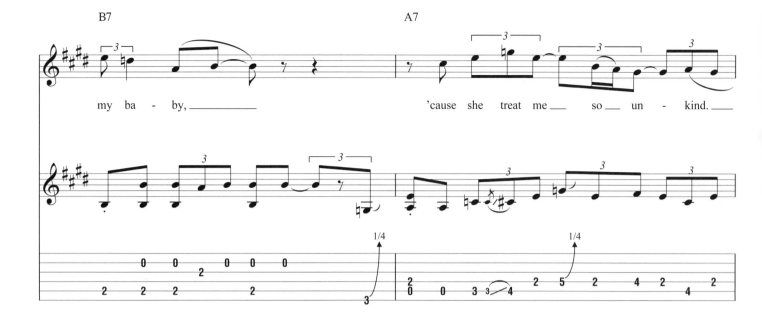

my ba - by, _____ 'cause she treat me ___ so ___ un - kind. ___

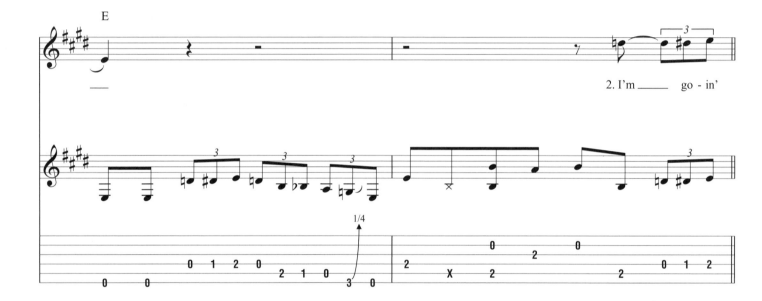

___ 2. I'm _____ go - in'

Verse

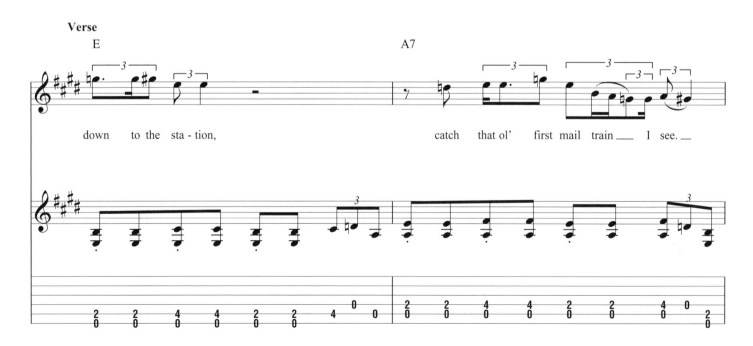

down   to the sta - tion,   catch   that ol'   first mail train ___ I see. ___

I'm ___ go - in'

down to the sta - tion, _____ catch that ol' first _ mail train _____ I see. _____

I ____ got de blues _

'bout Miss So and So,_____ an' the sun got the blues_____ 'bout me._____

let ring -

let ring - - - - -

Guitar Solo

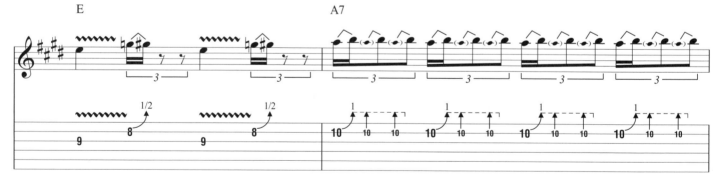

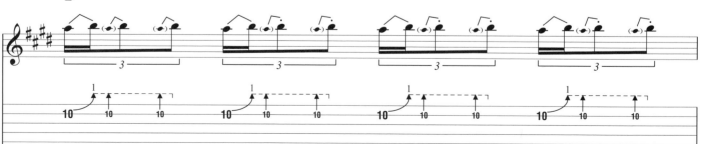

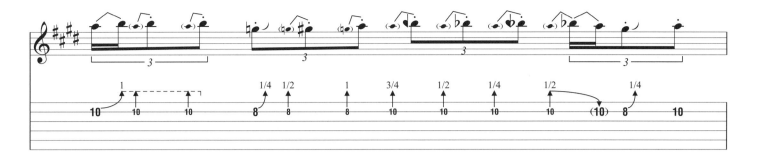

A7

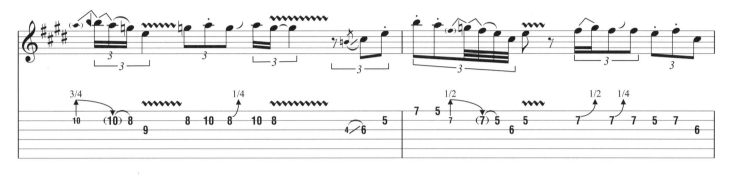

E

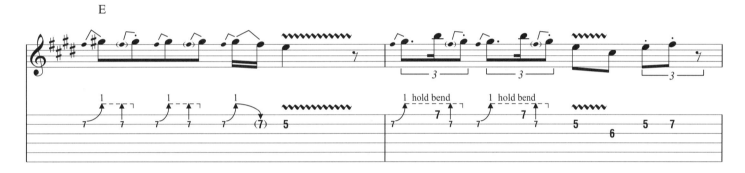

B7   A7

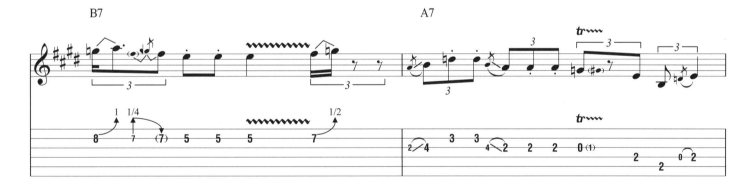

E

3. I got

Verse

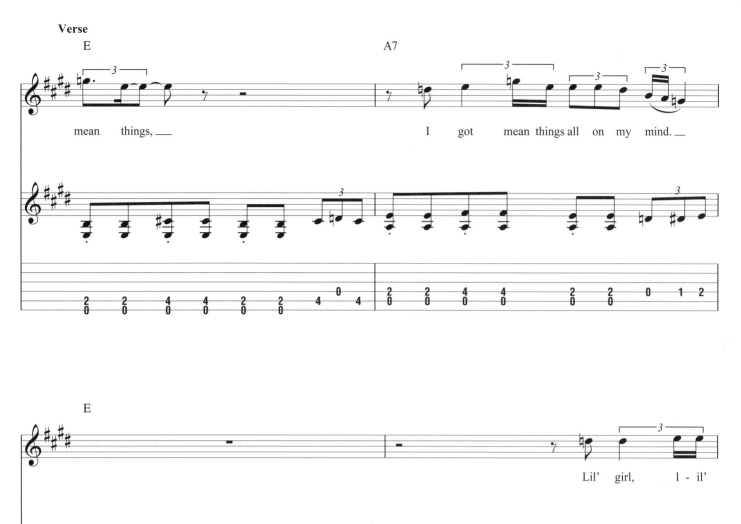

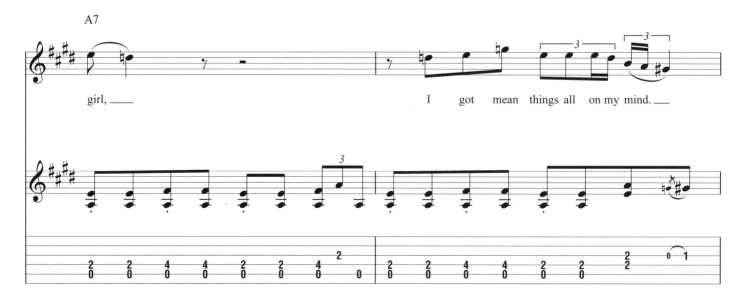

Is to leave

my ba - by, _____ 'cause she treat _ me so _ un - kind. _

Sweet Home Chicago

Words and Music by Robert Johnson

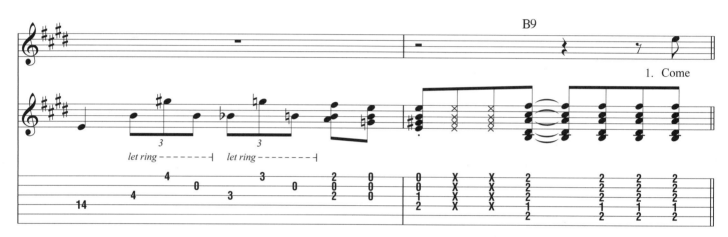

ba - by don't - cha wan - na go

back ___ to that

same old ___ place, ___ sweet home ___ Chi -

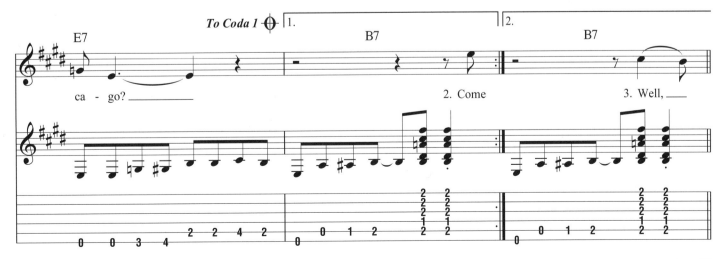

To Coda 1

1.

2.

ca - go? ___ 2. Come 3. Well, ___

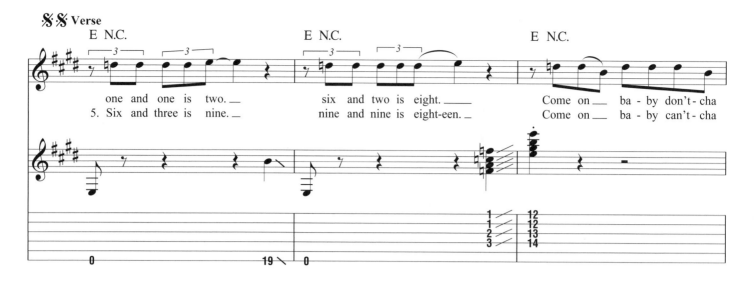

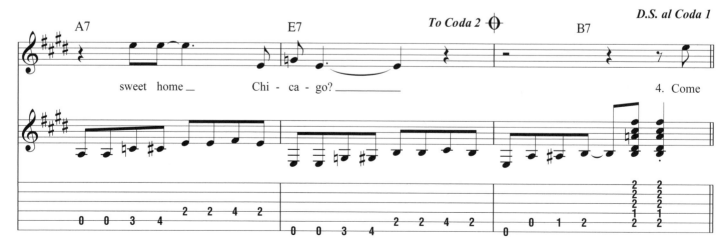

⊕ **Coda 1**

Guitar Solo

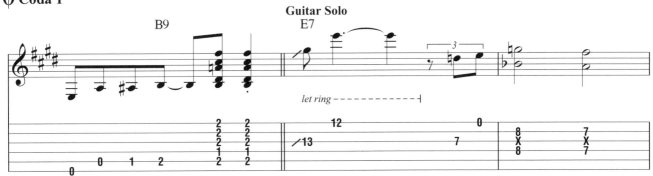

*Hammer from
nowhere. (Don't
pick.)

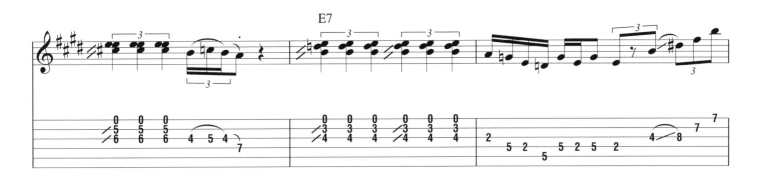

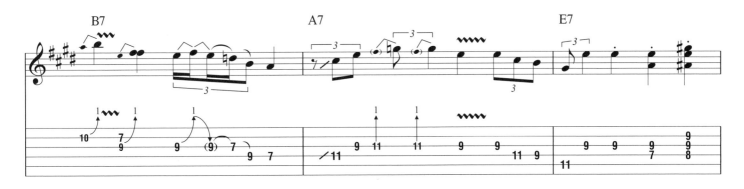

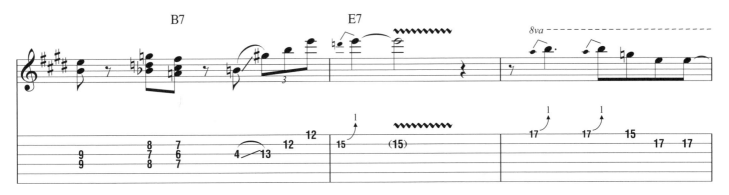

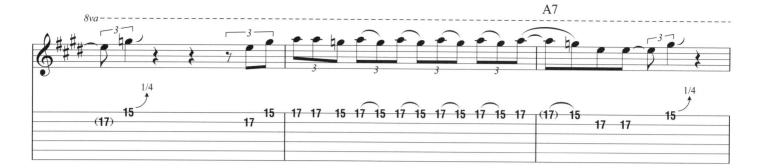

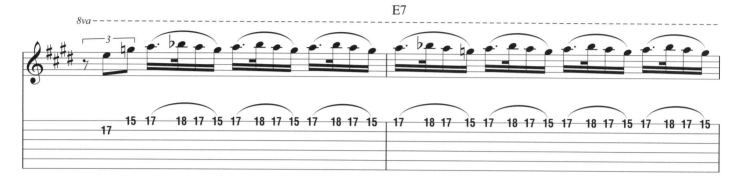

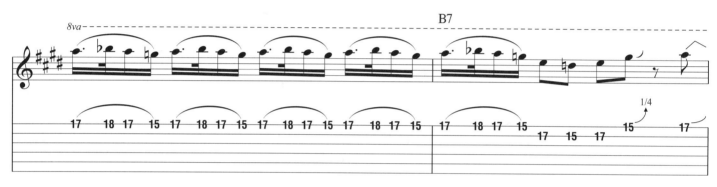

D.S.S. al Coda 2

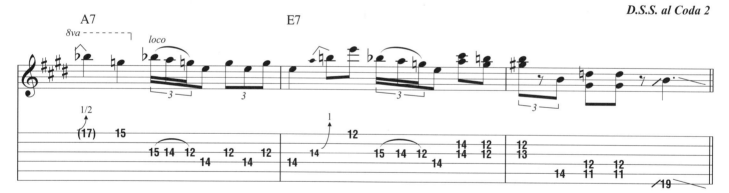

 Coda 2

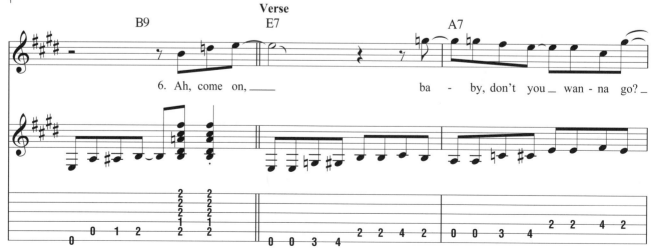

6. Ah, come on, _____ ba - by, don't you ___ wan - na go? ___

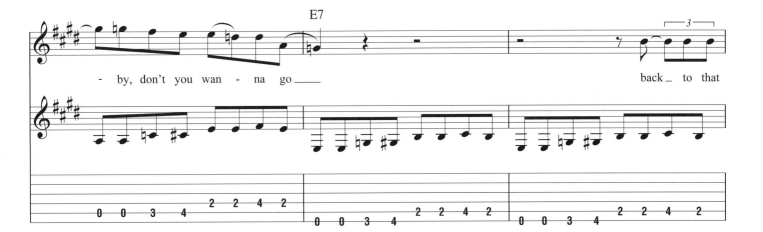

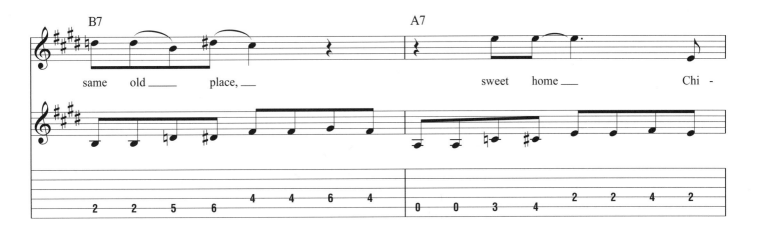

Travelling Riverside Blues

Words and Music by Robert Johnson, Jimmy Page and Robert Plant

Open G tuning:
(low to high) D-G-D-G-B-D

Intro
Moderately ♩ = 120

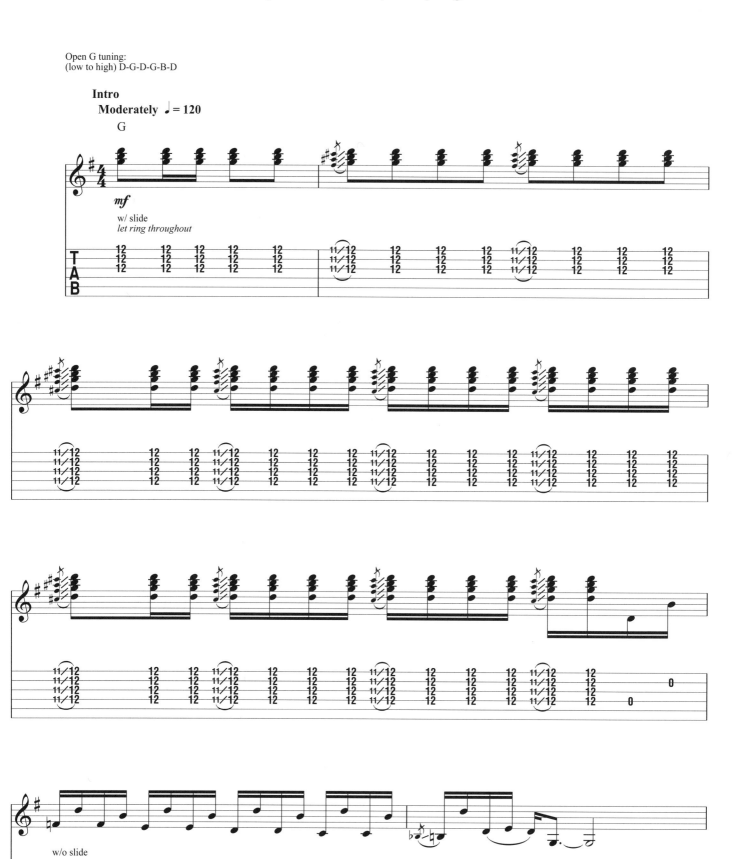

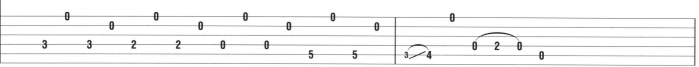

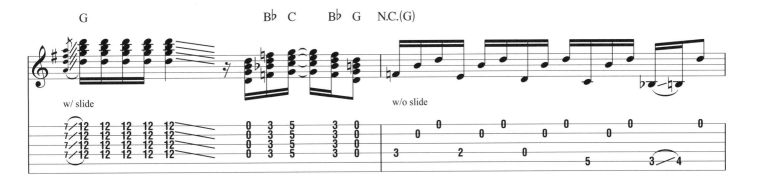

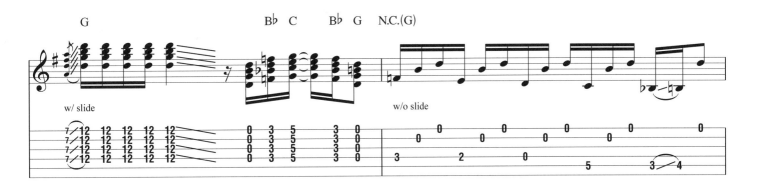

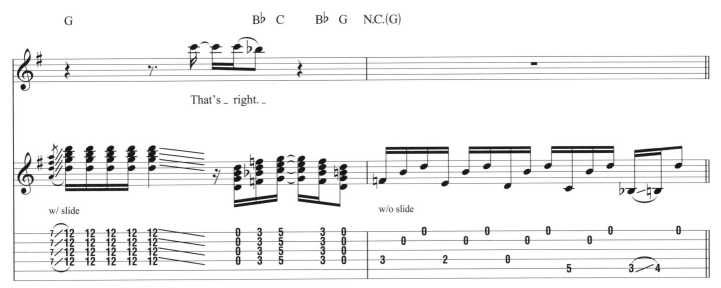

Verse

1. Asked sweet ma-ma, let __ me, ah, be her kid. __ She said, __ ah,

"You might get hurt __ if you __ don't ah, keep it hid." __ Well, I, _____

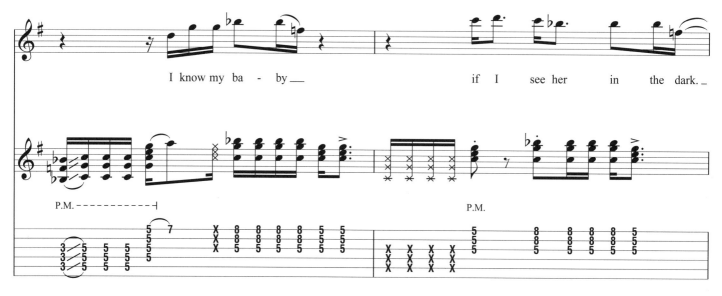

I know my ba - by __ if I see her in the dark. __

52

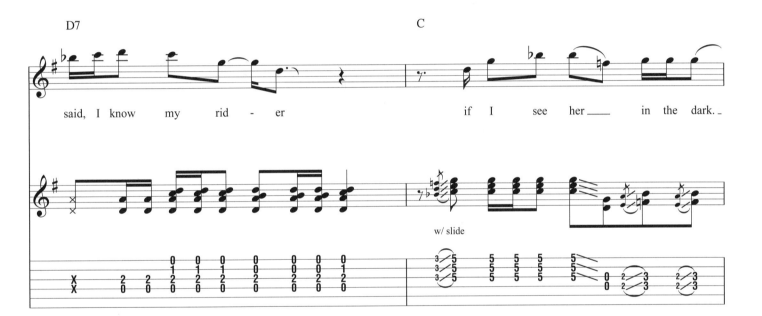

said, I know my rid - er   if I see her ___ in the dark. __

Now,

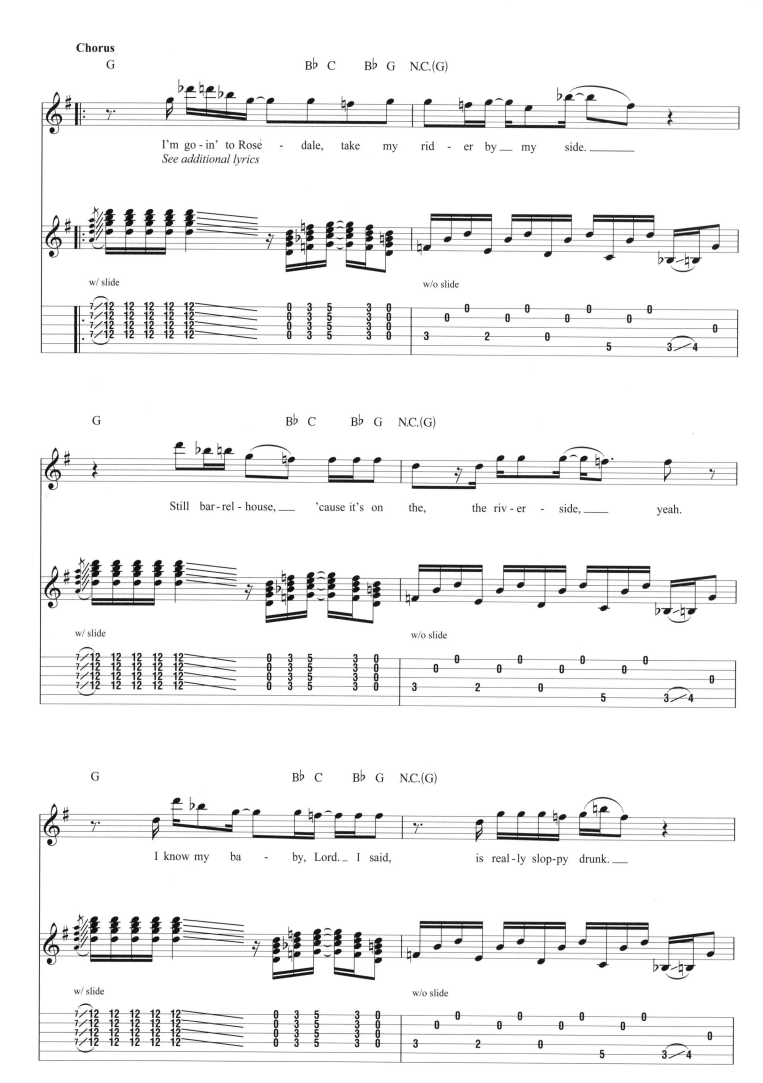

I know my ma - ma, Lord, a brown - skin, but she ain't no plum, _ ah, _ ha.

Verse

2. See my ba - by, tell _ her, tell her hur - ry home, _ ah.
3. *See additional lyrics*

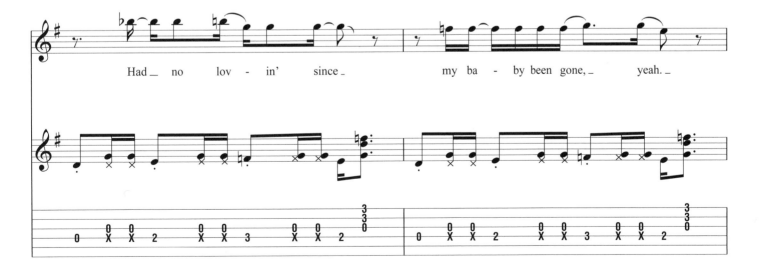

Had _ no lov - in' since _ my ba - by been gone, _ yeah. _

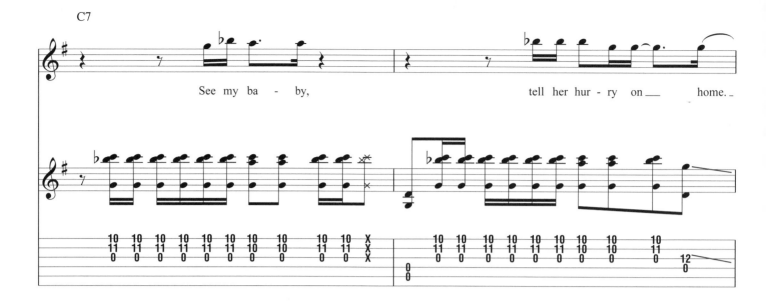

See my ba - by,   tell her hur - ry on ___ home. ___

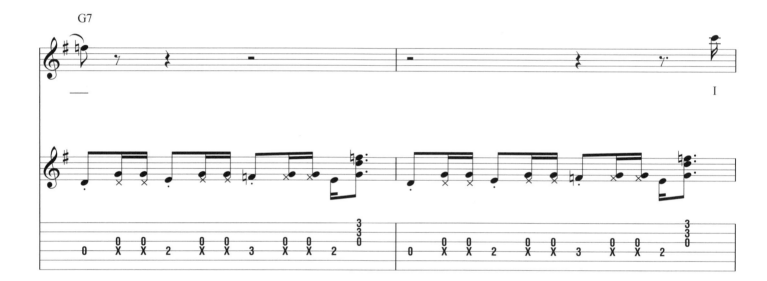

ain't had, Lord,   my right   mind ___   since my rid - er's ___

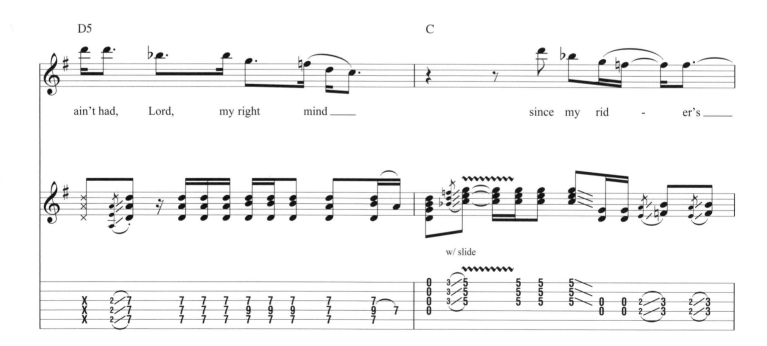

w/ slide

1.

G

___ been gone. ___ Hey.

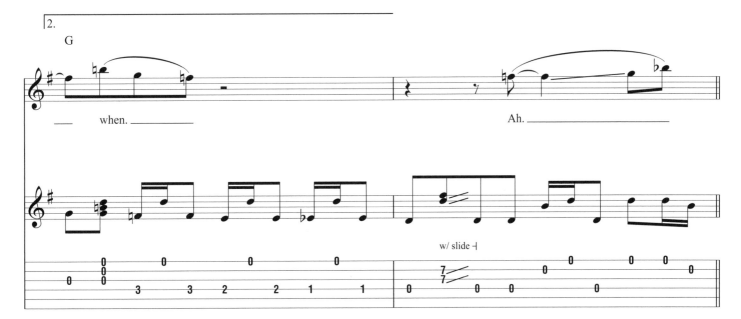

2.

G

___ when. ___ Ah. ___

Interlude

G   B♭ C   B♭ G N.C.(G)

Yeah. ___

w/ slide   w/o slide

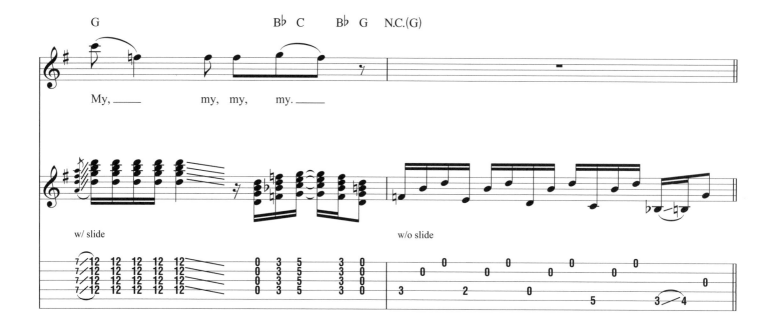

My, _____ my, my, my. _____

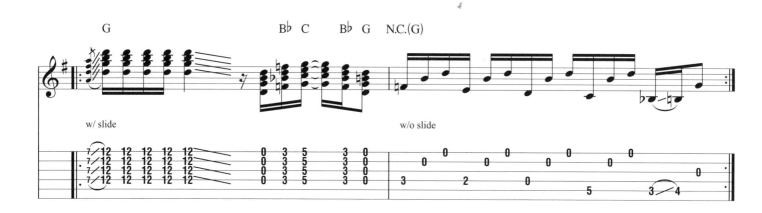

Guitar Solo

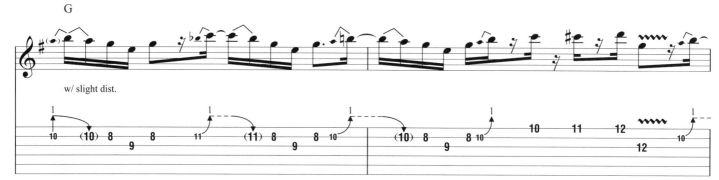

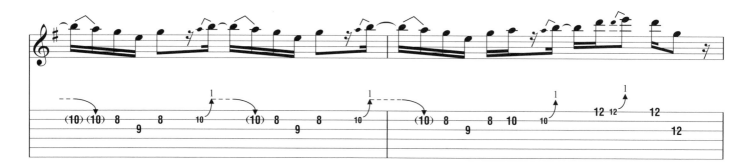

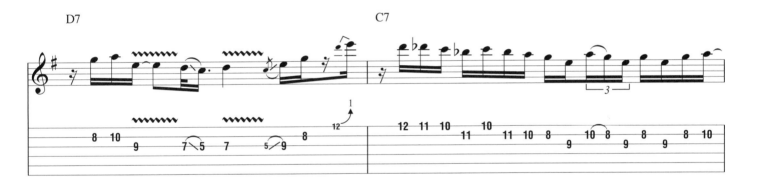

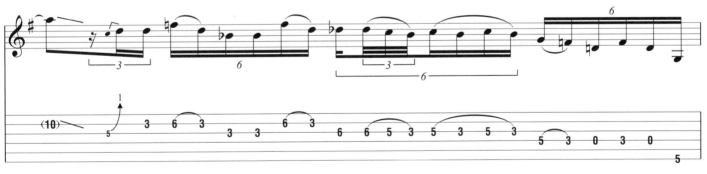

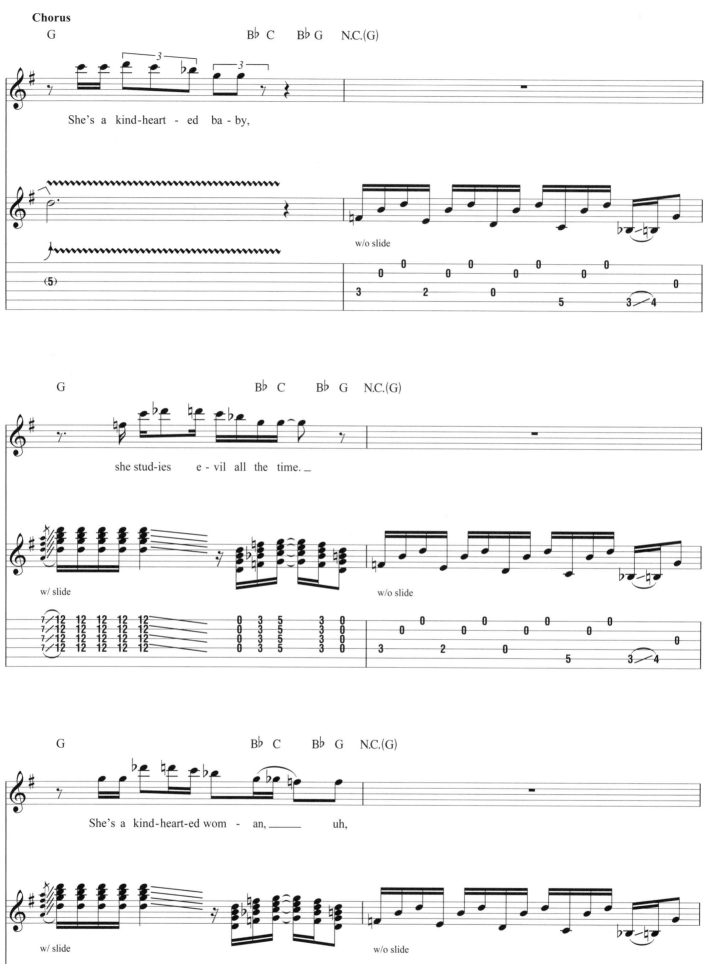

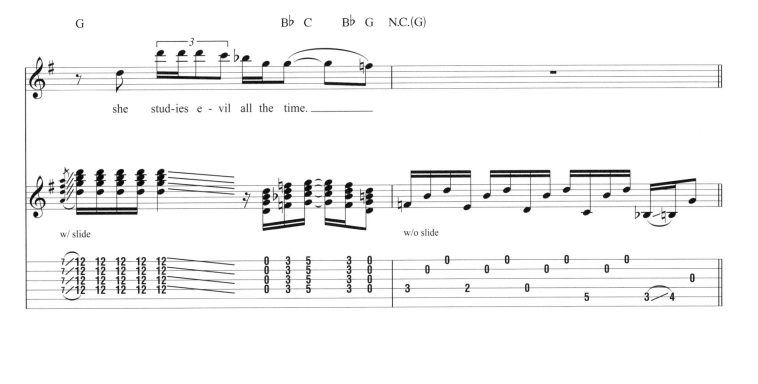

she stud-ies e - vil all the time.

w/ slide

w/o slide

Verse

G7

4. Squeeze my lem-on till the juice runs down my leg.

Squeeze it so hard I fall right out of bed. And you

squeeze ___ my lem-on   till the juice runs ___ down ___

___ my leg.   *Spoken:* I won-der if you know what I'm talk-ing a-bout.   Oh, but the

way   that you squeeze it girl, ___ uh,   I swear I'm ___ gon-na   fall right out of

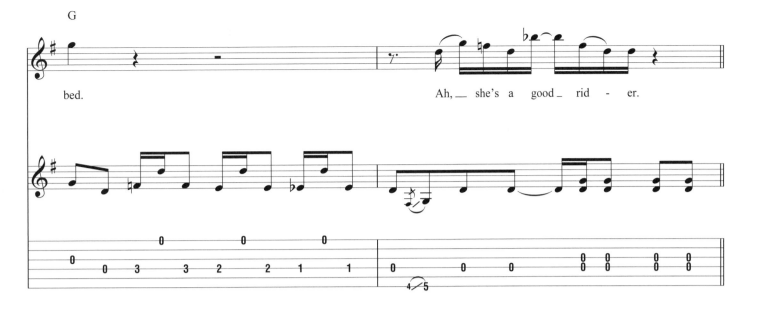

bed.

Ah, — she's a good — rid - er.

Outro

Hey, — yeah.

w/ slide   w/o slide

She's my kind - heart-ed ba - by.

w/ slide   w/o slide

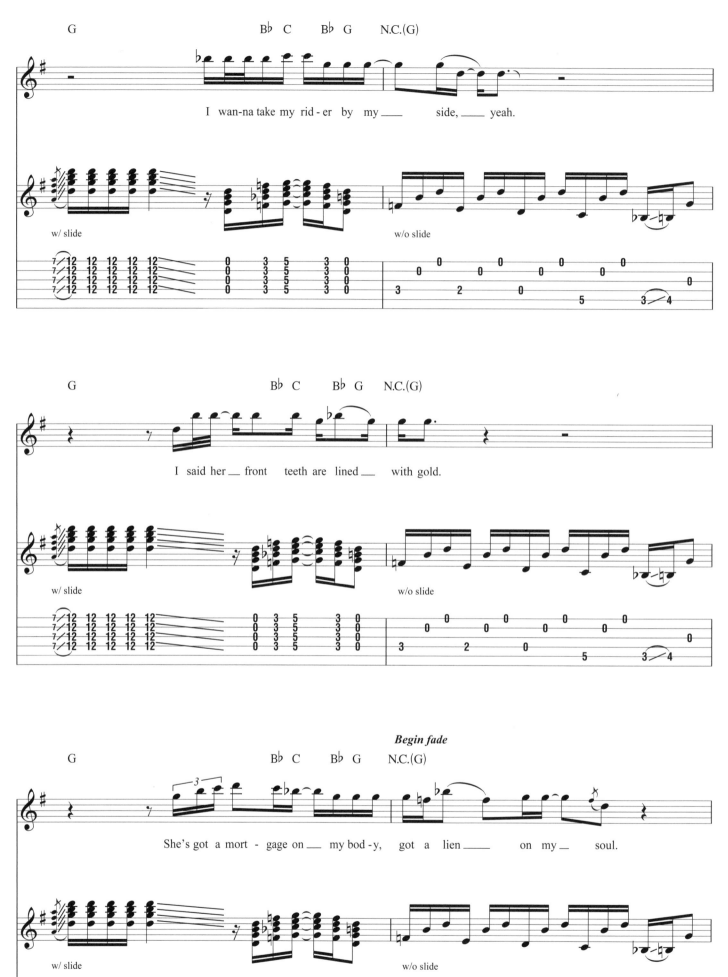

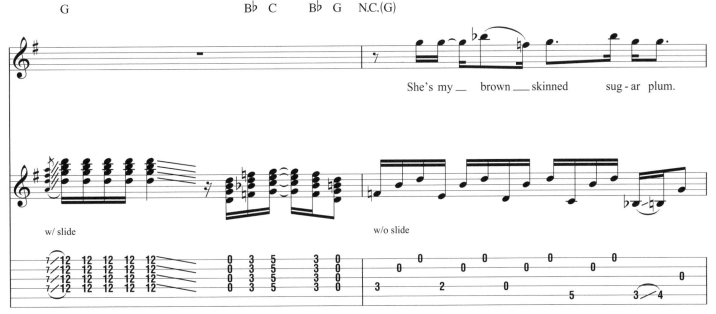

She's my __ brown __ skinned sug - ar plum.

w/ slide

w/o slide

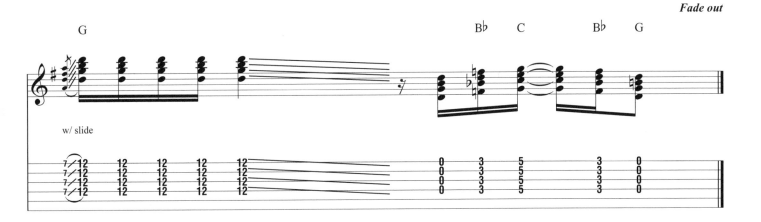

Fade out

w/ slide

Additional Lyrics

Chorus Promises she's my rider.
I wanna tell you she's my rider.
Know you're mine, she's my rider.
She ain't but sixteen, but she's my rider.

3. I'm goin' to Rosedale, take my rider by my side.
Anybody argue with me, man, I'll keep them satisfied.
Well, I see my baby. Tell her, tell her the shape I'm in.
Ain't had no lovin', Lord, since you know when.

Walkin' Blues

Words and Music by Robert Johnson

Open G tuning:
(low to high) D-G-D-G-B-D

Intro
Moderately ♩ = 104

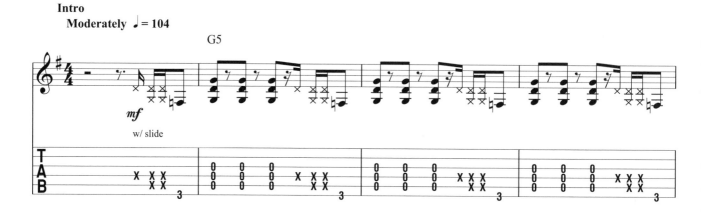

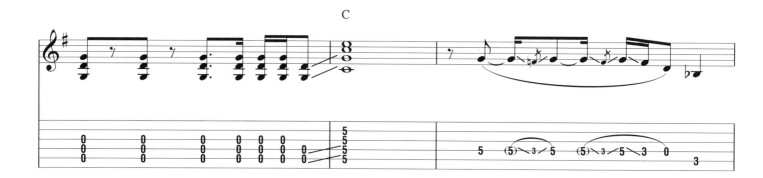

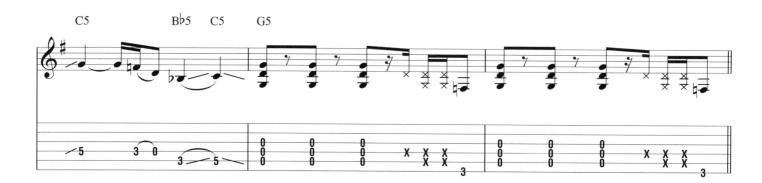

know 'bout___ that I got,___ yeah,___ these walk-ing blues.__

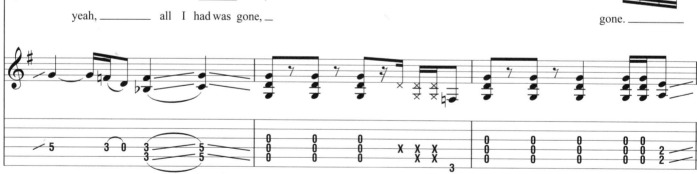

yeah,___ all I had was gone,__ gone.___

Guitar Solo

C

D.S. al Coda

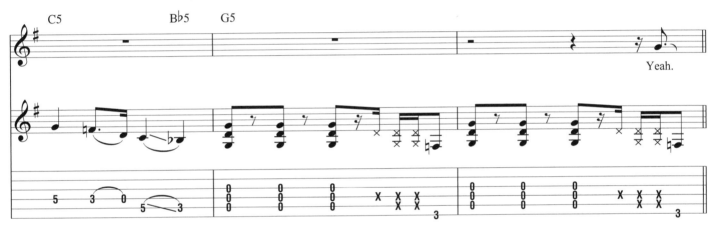

C5   Bb5   G5

Yeah.

⊕ Coda

C5   Bb5   C5   G5

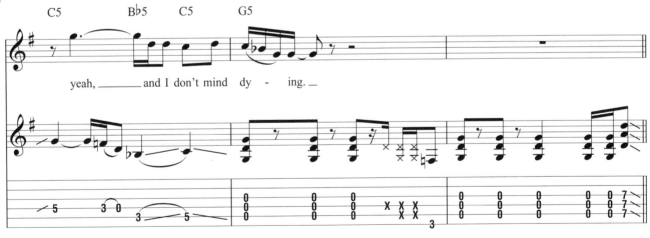

yeah, _____ and I don't mind dy - ing. __

Harmonica Solo

G5

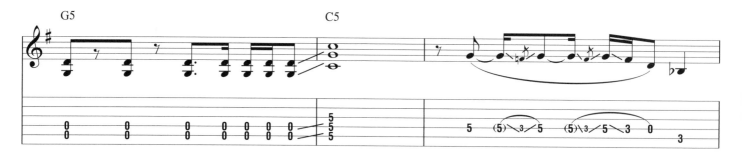

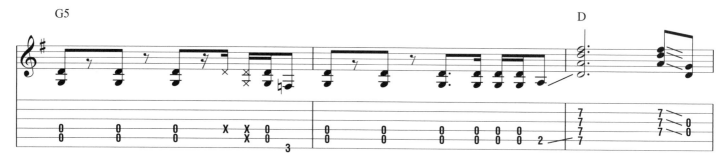

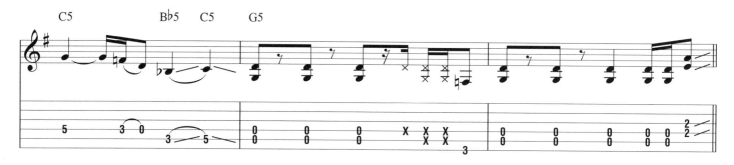

Guitar Solo

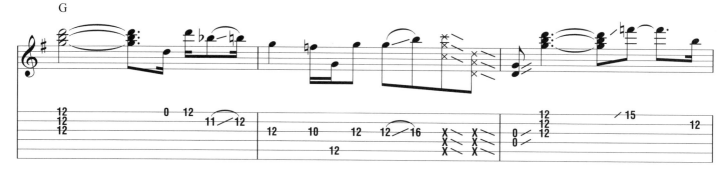

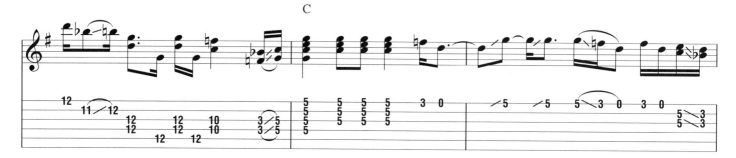

Free time

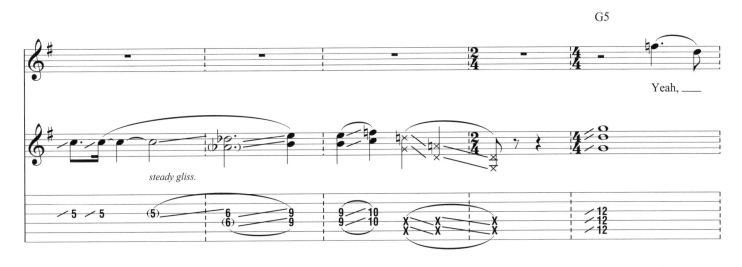

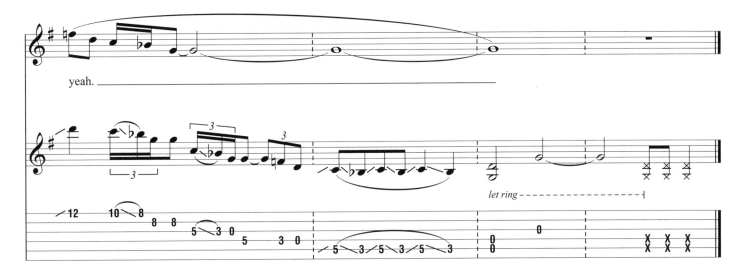

Additional Lyrics

2. And I feel like blowing the lonesome horn.
   Got up this morning, Bernice was gone.
   And I feel like blowing, yeah, my lonesome horn.
   Well, I got up this morning, yeah, all I had was gone, gone.

3. Leave this morning, ride them blinds.
   Been mistreated, darling, don't mind dying.
   And I'm leaving this morning, have to have them blinds.
   Yeah, I been mistreated now, baby,
   Yeah, and I don't mind dying.

I Believe I'll Dust My Broom

Words and Music by Robert Johnson

Open D tuning:
(low to high) D-A-D-F♯-A-D

Intro
Moderately ♩ = 124

N.C.(D7)

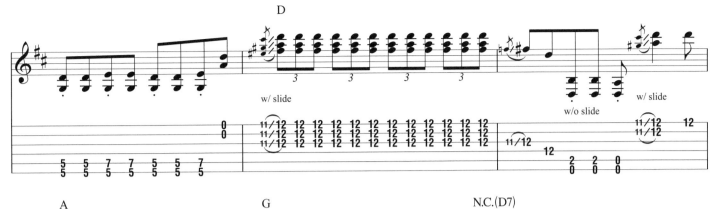

D

w/ slide

w/o slide

w/ slide

A

G

N.C.(D7)

w/o slide

let ring - - - 4   let ring - - - 4   let ring - - - 4

§ **Verse**

(A7)

D

1. I'm gon-na get up in the morn - in',

2., 3., 4. *See additional lyrics*

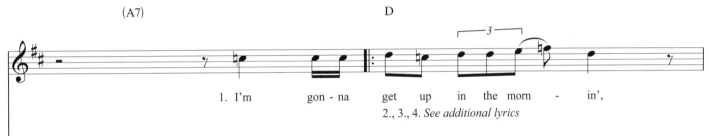

G

D

b'lieve I'll dust my _____ broom.

w/ slide

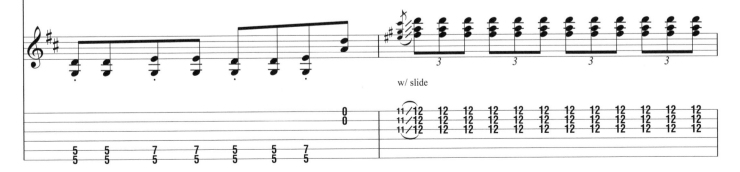

3rd & 4th times, substitute Fill 2

G

Gon - na get up in the morn - in',

w/o slide   w/ slide   w/o slide

D

b'lieve I'll dust my ____ broom.

w/ slide

2nd, 3rd & 4th times, substitute Fill 1

A

Well, I'm tired of tell - in' ya,

w/o slide   w/ slide   w/o slide

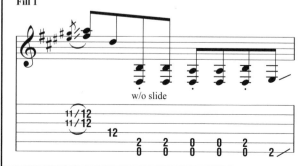

Fill 1

w/o slide

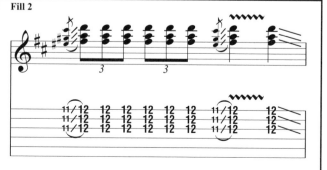

Fill 2

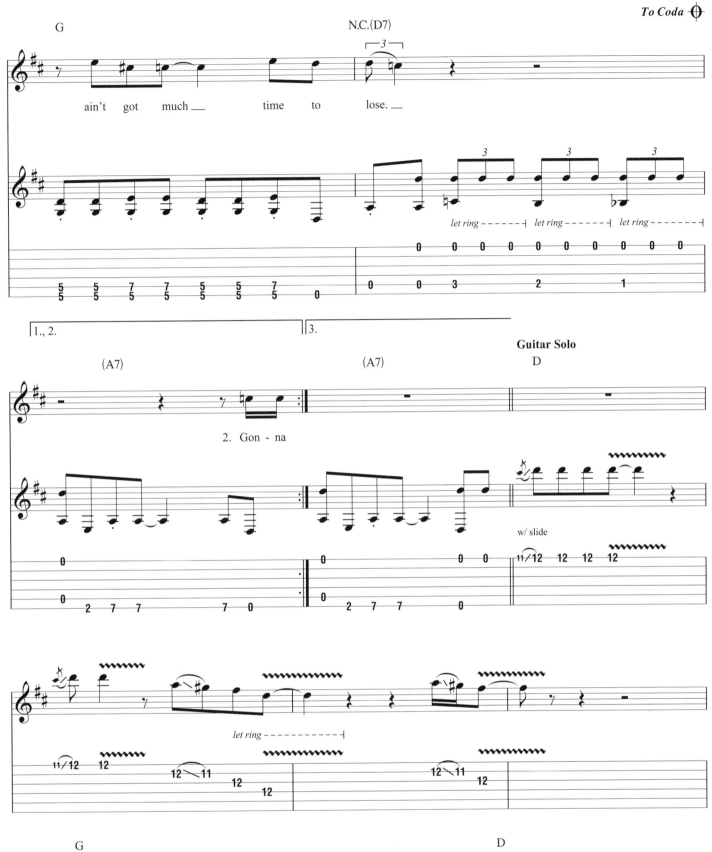

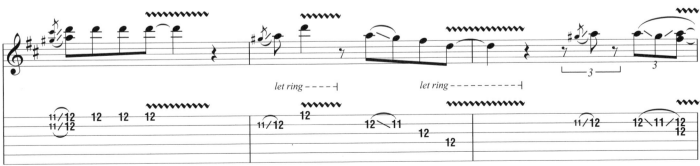

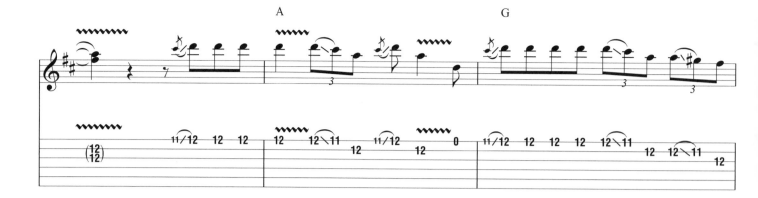

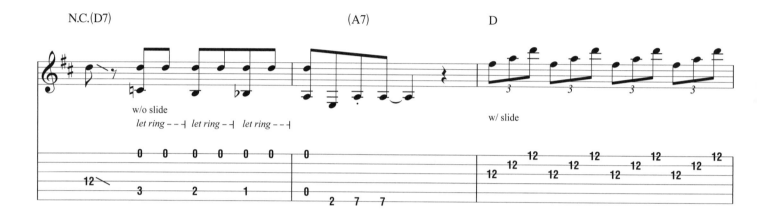

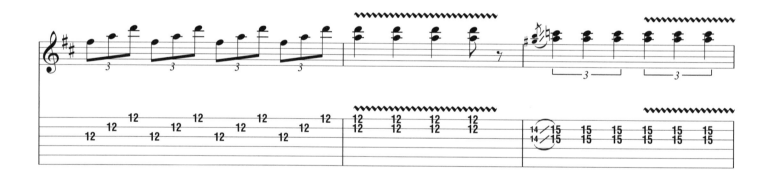

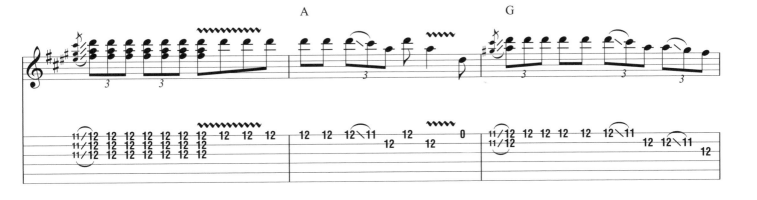

D.S. al Coda

⊕ Coda

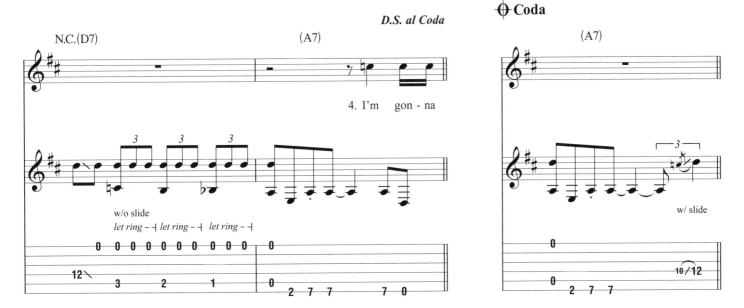

4. I'm gon - na

Outro-Guitar Solo

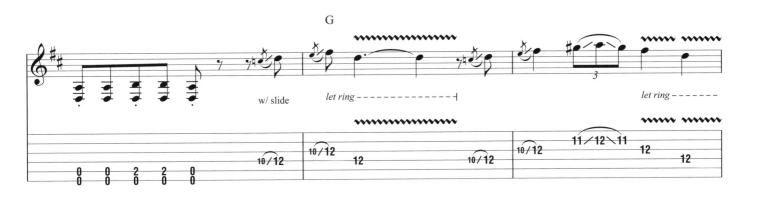

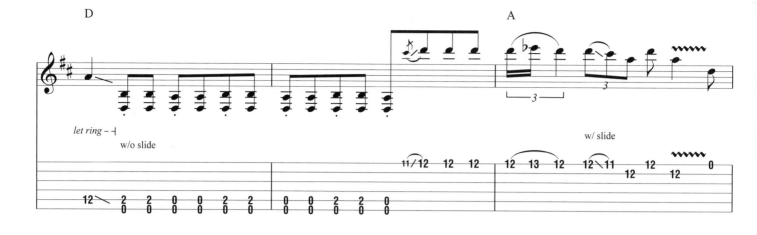

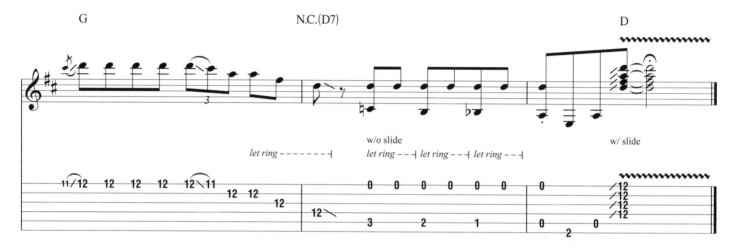

Additional Lyrics

2. Gonna write a letter, gonna send a special telegram.
   Gonna write a letter, gonna send a special telegram.
   I'm gonna find my baby, you know doggone well I am.

3. Well, believe, believe my time alone.
   I believe, believe my time alone.
   You gonna wake up in the mornin', find your good man gone.

4. I'm gonna call up China, see if my baby's over there.
   I'm gonna call up China, see if my baby's over there.
   Well, she's a fine little woman; she's in the world somewhere.